GRACE NOTES

GRACE NOTES

POEMS BY **RITA DOVE**

W · W · NORTON & COMPANY · NEW YORK · LONDON

Published simultaneously in Canada by Penguin Books Canada Ltd., 2801
John Street, Markham, Ontario L3R 1B4.
Printed in the United States of America.

The text of this book is composed in Devinne, with display type set in
Mannequin. Composition and manufacturing by The Haddon Craftsmen Inc.
Book design by Antonina Krass.

First Edition

Library of Congress Cataloging-in-Publication Data
Dove, Rita.
  Grace notes: poems/by Rita Dove.—1st ed.
    p. cm.
  I. Title.
PS3554.0884G7   1989
811'.54—dc19 89–30762

ISBN 0-393-02719-8

W. W. Norton & Company, Inc., 500 Fifth Avenue, New York, N. Y. 10110
W. W. Norton & Company Ltd., 37 Great Russell Street, London WC1B 3NU
1 2 3 4 5 6 7 8 9 0

Acknowledgments

The poems in *Grace Notes* first appeared, sometimes in different versions, in the following publications:

Black Scholar: "Poem in Which I Refuse Contemplation"; *The Boston Review:* "Flash Cards," "Saints"; *Caprice:* "Medusa"; *Chelsea:* "Dialectical Romance," "Particulars"; *Clockwatch Review:* "Mississippi," "Stitches"; *Cottonwood:* "Summit Beach, 1921"; *Erato:* "On the Road to Damascus"; *Five A.M.:* "After Reading *Mickey in the Night Kitchen* for the Third Time before Bed"; *The Georgia Review:* "Horse and Tree"; *Graham House Review:* "In the Museum," "Pastoral"; *Hayden's Ferry Review:* "After Storm"; *High Plains Literary Review:* "Backyard, 6 A.M.," "Ozone"; *The Iowa Review:* "Turning Thirty, I Contemplate Students Bicycling Home"; *The Michigan Quarterly Review:* "Arrow"; *Partisan Review:* "Crab-Boil"; *Ploughshares:* "Fantasy and Science Fiction," "Hully Gully," "Obbligato"; *Poetry:* "Ars Poetica," "The Breathing, The Endless News," "Old Folk's Home, Jerusalem," "The Wake"; *Poetry Now:* "Quaker Oats," "Silos"; *Prairie Schooner:* "The Buckeye," "The Other Side of the House"; *River Styx:* "Uncle Millet"; *South Coast Poetry Journal:* "Sisters"; *The Seneca Review:* "Your Death"; *The Southern Review:* "Dog Days, Jerusalem," "Fifth Grade Autobiography," "The Gorge"; *Southwest Review:* "À l'Opéra," "Lint," "The Royal Workshops"; *Telescope:* "Watching *Last Year at Marienbad* at Roger Haggerty's House in Auburn, Alabama"; *TriQuarterly:* "And Counting," "Canary," "Genie's Prayer under the Kitchen Sink," "In a Neutral City," The Island Women of Paris"; *The Yale Review:* "Dedication."

"Canary" and "After Reading *Mickey in the Night Kitchen* for the Third Time before Bed" were also published in *Early Ripening: American Women's Poetry Now,* edited by Marge Piercy, Pandora Press (New York & London, 1987).

"Backyard, 6 A.M.," "The Breathing, The Endless News," "Genetic Expedition," "Horse and Tree," "The Other Side of the House," "Pastoral," and "After Reading *Mickey in the Night Kitchen* for the Third Time before Bed" appeared with seven collotype-printed photographs by Tamarra Kaida in a fine press edition entitled *The Other Side of the House,* published by Pyracantha Press (Arizona State University, Tempe, Arizona) in 1988.

"Ozone" was also printed as a broadside with a lithograph by Ron Gasowski in *The Dance of Death,* a portfolio produced by John Risseeuw at Pyracantha Press in 1989.

The quotes introducing the five sections of this book are drawn from the following works: Toni Morrison, "The Site of Memory" (I.); David McFadden, *A Trip Around Lake Huron,* & Hélène Cixous, *Illa* (II.); Rita Dove, *The Other Side of the House* (III.); Claude McKay, "My House" (IV.); Cavafy, "The City" (V.).

The author wishes to express her gratitude to Arizona State University for a sabbatical leave that enabled her to write some of these poems, and to the Rockefeller Foundation for a magic month at the Bellagio Study and Conference Center, where *Grace Notes* took shape.

for Fred and Aviva, as always

CONTENTS

III

IV

V

GRACE NOTES

Summit Beach, 1921

The Negro beach jumped to the twitch
of an oil drum tattoo and a mandolin,
sweaters flying off the finest brown shoulders
this side of the world.

She sat by the fire, shawl moored
by a single fake cameo. She was cold,
thank you, she did not care to dance—
the scar on her knee winking
with the evening chill.

Papa had said don't be so fast,
you're all you've got. So she refused
to cut the wing, though she let the boys
bring her sassafras tea and drank it down
neat as a dropped hankie.

Her knee had itched in the cast
till she grew mean from bravery.
She could wait, she was gold.
When the right man smiled it would be
music skittering up her calf

like a chuckle. She could feel
the breeze in her ears like water,
like the air as a child when
she climbed Papa's shed and stepped off
the tin roof into blue,

with her parasol and invisible wings.

I

All water has a perfect memory and is forever trying to get back to where it was.

—Toni Morrison

Silos

Like martial swans in spring paraded against the city sky's
shabby blue, they were always too white and
suddenly there.

They were never fingers, never xylophones, although once
a stranger said they put him in mind of Pan's pipes
and all the lost songs of Greece. But to the townspeople
they were like cigarettes, the smell chewy and bitter
like a field shorn of milkweed, or beer brewing, or
a fingernail scorched over a flame.

No, no, exclaimed the children. They're a fresh packet of chalk,
dreading math work.

They were masculine toys. They were tall wishes. They
were the ribs of the modern world.

Fifth Grade Autobiography

I was four in this photograph fishing
with my grandparents at a lake in Michigan.
My brother squats in poison ivy.
His Davy Crockett cap
sits squared on his head so the raccoon tail
flounces down the back of his sailor suit.

My grandfather sits to the far right
in a folding chair,
and I know his left hand is on
the tobacco in his pants pocket
because I used to wrap it for him
every Christmas. Grandmother's hips
bulge from the brush, she's leaning
into the ice chest, sun through the trees
printing her dress with soft
luminous paws.

I am staring jealously at my brother;
the day before he rode his first horse, alone.
I was strapped in a basket
behind my grandfather.
He smelled of lemons. He's died—

but I remember his hands.

The Buckeye

We learned about the state tree
in school—its fruit
so useless, so ugly

no one bothered to
commend the smudged trunk
nor the slim leaves shifting

over our heads. Yet
they were a good thing to kick
along gutters

on the way home,
though they stank like
a drunk's piss in the roads

where cars had smashed
them. And in autumn
when the spiny helmets split

open,
there was the bald
seed with its wheat-

colored eye.
We loved
the modest countenance beneath

that leathery cap.
We, too, did not want to leave
our mothers.

We piled them up
for ammunition.
We lay down

with them
among the bruised leaves
so that we could

rise, shining.

The grain elevators have stood empty for years. They used to feed an entire nation of children. Hunched in red leatherette breakfast-nooks, fingers dreaming, children let their spoons clack on the white sides of their bowls. They stare at the carton on the table, a miniature silo with a kindly face smiling under a stiff black hat.

They eat their oats with milk and butter and sugar. They eat their oats in their sleep, where horsedrawn carts jolt along miry roads, past cabins where other children wait, half-frozen under tattered counterpanes. The man with the black hat, a burlap sack tucked under his arm, steps down from the wagon whispering *come out, don't be afraid.*

And they come, the sick and the healthy; the red, the brown, the white; the ruddy and the sallow; the curly and the lank. They tumble from rafters and crawl out of trundles. He gives them to eat. He gives them prayers and a good start in the morning. He gives them free enterprise; he gives them the flag and PA systems and roller skates and citizenship. He gives them a tawny canoe to portage overland, through the woods, through the midwestern snow.

Flash Cards

In math I was the whiz kid, keeper
of oranges and apples. *What you don't understand,*
master, my father said; the faster
I answered, the faster they came.

I could see one bud on the teacher's geranium,
one clear bee sputtering at the wet pane.
The tulip trees always dragged after heavy rain
so I tucked my head as my boots slapped home.

My father put up his feet after work
and relaxed with a highball and *The Life of Lincoln.*
After supper we drilled and I climbed the dark

before sleep, before a thin voice hissed
numbers as I spun on a wheel. I had to guess.
Ten, I kept saying, *I'm only ten.*

CRAB-BOIL

(Ft. Myers, 1962)

Why do I remember the sky
above the forbidden beach,
why only blue and the scratch,
shell on tin, of their distress?
The rest

imagination supplies:
bucket and angry pink beseeching
claws. Why does Aunt Helen
laugh before saying "Look at that—

a bunch of niggers, not
a-one get out 'fore the others pull him
back." I don't believe her—

just as I don't believe *they* won't come
and chase us back to the colored-only shore
crisp with litter and broken glass.

"When do we kill them?"
"Kill 'em? Hell, the water does *that.*
They don't feel a thing . . . no nervous system."

I decide to believe this: I'm hungry.
Dismantled, they're merely exotic,
a blushing meat. After all, she *has*
grown old in the South. If
we're kicked out now, I'm ready.

HULLY GULLY

Locked in bathrooms for hours,
daydreaming in kitchens
as they leaned their elbows
into the shells of lemons,

they were humming, they were humming
Hully Gully. Summer lasted

a long time; porch geraniums
rocked the grandmothers to sleep
as night slugged in, moon riding the sky
like a drop of oil on water. Then down
the swollen pitch of avenue
discourteous blouses, bright rifflings,
gum popping to an invisible beat,

daughters floating above the ranks of bobby socks.
Theirs was a field to lie down in
while fathers worked swing shift and
wives straightened oval photographs
above the exhausted chenille
in bedrooms upstairs everywhere. . . .

On my knees in the dark I looked out
the front door of my parents' house
and across the street saw an identical
stoop, the porthole glass
wreathed in pine boughs with a flat red bow.
I knew if I crossed the street and entered,
taking living room, stairwell and landing
in reverse, I'd end up on my knees
in a house my parents never owned nor dreamed of owning
in the dark not daring
to open my eyes.

*

The skyscraper was happy
alone, willow-like
on the edge of the frontier,
nestled in oak and Iroquois.
Its elevators whooshed and chimed
and the sky ionized indigo, readied
for storm. Moccasins inched closer
while far away in a field,
Ben and his silver key make history
and the skyscraper, suddenly aware
of its goofy reverie,
is swallowed into mud like a godhead.

*

Give the village idiot back
his rose, why tease a stupid boy?
So what if it's a full-blown green?
Children are always imagining things.
Sometimes, shutting a book and rising,
you can walk off the back porch
and into the sea—though
it's not the sort of story
you'd tell your mother.

SISTERS

for Robin Dove Waynesboro

This is the one we called
Bird of the Dead, Double Bird
Who Feeds on Carrion. Dark
with a red organdy dress
for her third birthday,
she cried and cried,
snap-eyed imp whose brow sprouted horns
whenever she screwed up her face.

"Buzzard!" we shrieked
and when that was forbidden:
"Schmawk Schmawk Bird!" after the local radio
personality. Several beatings later
the first literary effort appeared, a story
called "Blank the Buzzard,"
for which I claimed the First Amendment.
It was confiscated and shredded.

I can't believe she's taller
than me now, that my smile
lines sag where her Indian cheekbones soar.
This is my home, my knothole
we're posing in front of. The palm tree
throws a boa across our shoulders.
Light seals the cracks.

UNCLE MILLET

He'd slip a rubber band around a glass of rye,
pluck it with one pearly nail
like a song he couldn't get off his mind.

Twice-widowed, down from Toronto to cool his heels,
he kept up the tales of nylons
stuffed hastily into coat pockets,
an aproned great-aunt settling
her bulk onto the front porch swing
just as Baby Sister vaulted the backyard gate. . . .

Sure, he was no good. And I wasn't
allowed over when he pulled into town.
But I memorized the stories, imagining
Canada full of men who'd use
a knife to defend their right to say:

Man, she was butter
just waiting to melt.

POEM IN WHICH I
REFUSE CONTEMPLATION

A letter from my mother was waiting:
read in standing, one a.m.,
just arrived at my German mother-in-law

six hours from Paris by car.
Our daughter hops on Oma's bed,
happy to be back in a language

she knows. *Hello, all! Your postcard*
came on the nineth—familiar misspelled
words, exclamations. I wish my body

wouldn't cramp and leak; I want to—
as my daughter says, pretending to be
"Papa"—pull on boots and go for a long walk

alone. *Your cousin Ronnie in D.C.—*
remember him?—he was the one
a few months younger than you—

was strangulated at some chili joint,
your Aunt May is beside herself!
Mom skips to the garden which is

producing—onions, swiss chard,
lettuce, lettuce, lettuce, turnip greens and more lettuce
so far! The roses are flurishing.

Haven't I always hated gardening? And German,
with its patient, grunting building blocks,
and for that matter, English, too,

Americanese's chewy twang? *Raccoons
have taken up residence*
we were ten *in the crawl space*

but I can't feel his hand *who knows*
anymore *how we'll get them out?*
I'm still standing. Bags to unpack.

That's all for now. Take care.

II

The legendary forbidden fruit is the self.

—DAVID MCFADDEN

To inhabit was the most natural joy when I was still living inside; all was garden and I had not lost the way in.

—HÉLÈNE CIXOUS

MISSISSIPPI

In the beginning was the dark
moan and creak, a sidewheel
moving through. Thicker
then, scent of lilac,
scent of thyme; slight hairs
on a wrist lying down in sweat.
We were falling down
river, carnal
slippage and shadow melt.
We were standing on the deck
of the New World, before maps:
tepid seizure of a breeze
and the spirit hissing away . . .

After Storm

Already the desert sky had packed
its scarves and gone over the hard blue hills
when I awoke, throat
raw from the tail end of a dream
through which your cough and
the smoke of a cigarette sailed. I followed
the deep light of the hallway out

to where the patio roof gaped,
bamboo shades mocking the palm tree
in splintery arpeggios. You stood
flicking ash onto the trampled grass.
I could smell the rain leaving, the sage
enthralled in a bitter virtue for hours.

WATCHING *LAST YEAR AT MARIENBAD* AT ROGER HAGGERTY'S HOUSE IN AUBURN, ALABAMA

There is a corridor of light
through the pines, lint from the Spanish Moss.
There is the fallen sun
like ice and the twit of hidden birds
in our common backyards,
snakes threading the needles.

I walk the block past
Krogers with its exhausted wives
hovering over bins of frozen pork.

No one else has shown but their chairs are here.

We sit flanking the projector.
The opening sequence reminds Roger's
three-year-old daughter
of the wedding cake she ate last week.
It reminds me of my first train in Europe,
the windows, soft implosions
at the entrance of tunnels,
air carving its intricate laces. . . .

The child has fallen asleep with a doll
on the sagging couch.

Here, nothing's mysterious—books and
newspapers. The first time
for anything is the best,
because there is no memory
linking its regrets to drop
like bracelets in the grass. What

a shabby monstrosity spring
actually is! Remember
that park bench, the frail wisteria. . . .

DOG DAYS, JERUSALEM

Exactly at six every evening I go
into the garden to wait for rain.
I'd been told it would come at six
if at all—but the sky goes matte,
so I turn on the sprinklers and follow
the lizard's woven escape
as water falls through itself like pity.

How tiny this broken applause!
In the library, beneath the fluted lamp,
I have set out black tea and oranges—
carefully, though no one will see me.
Night comes in on the clear register
of the *shofar,*
poor relative blowing its children home.

O z o n e

... Does the cosmic
space we dissolve into taste of us, then?

—Rilke; *The Second Elegy*

Everything civilized will whistle before
it rages—kettle of the asthmatic,
the aerosol can and its immaculate awl
perforating the dome of heaven.

We wire the sky for comfort;
we thread it through our lungs for a perfect fit.
We've arranged this calm, though it is constantly
unraveling.

> *Where does it go then,*
> *atmosphere suckered up*
> *an invisible flue?*
> *How can we know where it goes?*

A gentleman pokes blue through a buttonhole.

> *Rising, the pulse*
> *sings:*
> *memento mei*

The sky is wired so it won't fall down.
Each house notches into its neighbor
and then the next, the whole row scaldingly white,
unmistakable as a set of bared teeth.

to pull the plug
to disappear into an empty bouquet

If only we could lose ourselves
in the wreckage of the moment! Forget
where we stand, dead center, and
look up, look up,
track a falling star . . .

              now you see it

                      now you don't

Turning Thirty, I
Contemplate Students
Bicycling Home

This is the weather of change
and clear light. This is
weather on its B side,
askew, that propels
the legs of young men
in tight jeans wheeling

through the tired, wise
spring. Crickets too
awake in choirs
out of sight, although
I imagine we see
the same thing
and for a long way.

This, then, weather
to start over.
Evening rustles
her skirts of sulky
organza. Skin
prickles, defining
what is and shall not be. . . .

How private
the complaint of these
green hills.

PARTICULARS

She discovered she felt better
if the simplest motions
had their origin in agenda—
second coffee at nine or eating just
the top half of the muffin, no butter
with blueberry jam. She caught herself
crying every morning, ten sharp, as if
the weather front had swerved,
a titanic low pressure system
moving in as night steamed off
and left a day with nothing else
to fill it but moisture. She wept
steadily, and once
she recognized the pattern,
took care to be in one spot waiting
a few moments before. They weren't
tears of relief, and after a few weeks
not even of a particular sorrow.
*We never learn a secret until
it's useless,* she thought, and perhaps
that was what she was weeping over:
the lack of conclusion,
the eternal *dénouement.*

YOUR DEATH

On the day that will always belong to you,
lunar clockwork had faltered
and I was certain. Walking
the streets of Manhattan I thought:
Remember this day. I felt already
like an urn, filling with wine.

To celebrate, your son and I
took a stroll through Bloomingdale's
where he developed a headache
among the copper skillets and
tiers of collapsible baskets.
Pain tracked us through
the china, driving us
finally to the subway
and home,

where the phone was ringing
with bad news. Even now,
my new daughter
asleep in the crib, I can't shake
the moment his headache stopped
and the day changed ownership.
I felt robbed. Even the first
bite of the tuna fish sandwich
I had bought at the corner
became yours.

THE WAKE

Your absence distributed itself
like an invitation.
Friends and relatives
kept coming, trying
to fill up the house.
But the rooms still gaped—
the green hanger swang empty, and
the head of the table
demanded a plate.

When I sat down in the armchair
your warm breath fell
over my shoulder.
When I climbed to bed I walked
through your blind departure.
The others stayed downstairs,
trying to cover
the silence with weeping.

When I lay down between the sheets
I lay down in the cool waters
of my own womb
and became the child
inside, innocuous
as a button, helplessly growing.
I slept because it was the only
thing I could do. I even dreamed.
I couldn't stop myself.

III

Where's a word, a talisman, to hold against the world?

THE OTHER SIDE OF THE HOUSE

*But it wasn't a dream; it was a place! And you
. . . and you . . . and you . . . and you were there!*

—Dorothy, in *The Wizard of Oz*

I walk out the kitchen door
trailing extension cords into the open
gaze of the Southwest—

the green surreptitious,
dusty like a trenchcoat.

From the beautiful lawnmower
float curls of evaporated gasoline;
the hinged ax of the butterfly pauses.

Where am I in the stingy
desert broom, where
in the blank soul of the olive?
I hear the sand preparing to flee. . . .

Many still moments,
aligned, repair
the thin split of an afternoon—
its orange fiction, the dim
aggression of my daughter on the terrace drawing
her idea of a home. Somewhere

I learned to walk out of a thought
and not snap back the way
railroad cars telescope into a train.

The sand flies so fast, it leaves no shadow.

37

PASTORAL

Like an otter, but warm,
she latched onto the shadowy tip
and I watched, diminished
by those amazing gulps. Finished
she let her head loll, eyes
unfocused and large: milk-drunk.

I liked afterwards best, lying
outside on a quilt, her new skin
spread out like meringue. I felt then
what a young man must feel
with his first love asleep on his breast:
desire, and the freedom to imagine it.

Horse and Tree

Everybody who's anybody longs to be a tree—
or ride one, hair blown to froth.
That's why horses were invented, and saddles
tooled with singular stars.

This is why we braid their harsh manes
as if they were children, why children
might fear a carousel at first for the way
it insists that life is round. No,

we reply, there is music and then it stops;
the beautiful is always rising and falling.
We call and the children sing back *one more time.*
In the tree the luminous sap ascends.

The Breathing, The Endless News

Every god is lonely, an exile
composed of parts: elk horn,
cloven hoof. Receptacle

for wishes, each god is empty
without us, penitent,
raking our yards into windblown piles. . . .

Children know this: they are
the trailings of gods. Their eyes
hold nothing at birth then fill slowly

with the myth of ourselves. Not so the dolls,
out for the count, each toe pouting from
the slumped-over toddler clothes:

no blossoming there. So we
give our children dolls, and
they know just what to do—

line them up and shoot them.
With every execution
doll and god grow stronger.

A FTER R EADING *M ICKEY IN THE N IGHT K ITCHEN* FOR THE T HIRD T IME B EFORE B ED

I'm in the milk and the milk's in me! . . . I'm Mickey!

My daughter spreads her legs
to find her vagina:
hairless, this mistaken
bit of nomenclature
is what a stranger cannot touch
without her yelling. She demands
to see mine and momentarily
we're a lopsided star
among the spilled toys,
my prodigious scallops
exposed to her neat cameo.

And yet the same glazed
tunnel, layered sequences.
She is three; that makes this
innocent. *We're pink!*
she shrieks, and bounds off.

Every month she wants
to know where it hurts
and what the wrinkled string means
between my legs. *This is good blood*
I say, but that's wrong, too.
How to tell her that it's what makes us—
black mother, cream child.
That we're in the pink
and the pink's in us.

GENETIC EXPEDITION

Each evening I see my breasts
slacker, black-tipped
like the heavy plugs on hot water bottles;
each day resembling more the spiked fruits
dangling from natives in the *National Geographic*
my father forbade us to read.

Each morning I drip coffee onto my blouse
and tear into one slice of German bread,
thin layer of margarine, radishes, the years
spreading across my dark behind, even more
sumptuous after childbirth, the part of me
I swore to relish

always. My child has
her father's hips, his hair
like the miller's daughter, combed gold.
Though her lips are mine, housewives
stare when we cross the parking lot
because of that ghostly profusion.

You can't be cute, she says. *You're big.*
She's lost her toddler's belly,
that seaworthy prow. She regards me
with serious eyes, power-lit,
atomic gaze
I'm sucked into, sheer through to

the gray brain of sky.

BACKYARD, 6 A.M.

Nudged by bees, morning brightens to detail:
purple trumpets of the sage dropped
to the floor of the world. I'm back
home, jet lag and laundry,
space stapled down with every step. . . .

I swore to be good and the plane didn't
fall out of the sky. Is there such a thing
as a warning? I swear

I hear wings, and spiders
quickening in the forgotten shrines,
unwinding
each knot of grief,
each snagged insistence.

IV

I know the dark delight of being strange,
The penalty of difference in the crowd,
The loneliness of wisdom among fools . . .

—CLAUDE MCKAY

DEDICATION

after Czesław Miłosz

Ignore me. This request is knotted—
I'm not ashamed to admit it.
I won't promise anything. I am a magic
that can deafen you like a rainstorm or a well.

I am clear on introductions, the five minute flirt,
the ending of old news.
Broken color, this kind of wanting,
its tawdriness, its awkward uncertainties.

Once there was a hill thick with red maples
and a small brook
emerging from black briars.
There was quiet: no wind
to snatch the cries of birds flung above
where I sat and didn't know you yet.

What are music or books if not ways
to trap us in rumors? The freedom of fine cages!
I did not want bad music, I did not want
faulty scholarship; I wanted only to know

what I had missed, early on—
that ironic half-salute of the truly lost.

Thirty miles to the only decent restaurant
was nothing, a blink
in the long dull stare of Wyoming.
Halfway there the unknown but terribly
important essayist yelled Stop!
I wanna be *in* this; and walked
fifteen yards onto the land
before sky bore down and he came running,
crying Jesus—there's nothing out there!

I once met an Australian novelist
who told me he never learned to cook
because it robbed creative energy.
What he wanted most was
to be mute; he stacked up pages;
he entered each day with an ax.

What I want is this poem to be small,
a ghost town
on the larger map of wills.
Then you can pencil me in as a hawk:
a traveling x-marks-the-spot.

ARROW

The eminent scholar "took the bull by the horns,"
substituting urban black speech for the voice
of an illiterate cop in Aristophanes' *Thesmophoriazusae.*
And we sat there.
Dana's purple eyes deepened, Becky
twitched to her hairtips
and Janice in her red shoes
scribbled *he's an arschloch; do you want*
to leave? He's a model product of his
education, I scribbled back; *we can learn from this.*

So we sat through the applause
and my chest flashed hot, a void
sucking at my guts until I was all
flamed surface. I would have to speak up.
Then the scholar progressed

to his prize-winning translations of
the Italian Nobel Laureate. He explained the poet
to us: immense difficulty
with human relationships; sensitive;
women were a scrim through which he could see
heaven.
We sat through it. Quite lovely, these poems.
We could learn from them although they were saying
you women are nothing, nothing at all.

When the moment came I raised my hand,
phrased my question as I had to: sardonic,
eminently civil my condemnation
phrased in the language of fathers—

felt the room freeze behind me.
And the answer came as it had to:
humanity—celebrate our differences—
the virility of ethnicity. My students
sat there already devising

their different ways of coping:
Dana knowing it best to have
the migraine at once, get the poison out quickly
Becky holding it back for five hours   and Janice
making it to the evening reading and
party afterwards
in black pants and tunic with silver mirrors
her shoes pointed and studded, wicked witch shoes:
Janice who will wear red for three days or
yellow brighter
than her hair so she can't be
seen   at all

STITCHES

When skin opens
where a scar
should be, I think nothing but
"So I *am* white underneath!"
Blood swells then
dribbles into the elbow.

All that preparation for nothing!
I phone the university
to explain. My husband
storms in, motor running,
pales, and packs me off to Emergency.

> *Wear a red dress for the first time*
> *in a year, and look what happens.*
> *You were on your way to class,*
> *you had a plane to catch after—*
> *the bulging suitcase knocked you off-center.*

The doctor's teeth are beavery, yellow:
he whistles as he works, as topsoil
puckers over its wound. Amazing
there's no pain—just pressure
as the skin's tugged up by his thread

like a trout, a black line straight
from a seamstress' nightmare: foot-tread
pedalling the needle right through.

> *You just can't stop being witty, can you?*

Oh, but I can. I always could.

In the Museum

a boy, at most
sixteen.

Besieged by the drums
and flags of youth,
brilliant gravity
and cornucopian stone

retreat.
The Discus Thrower
(reproduction)
stares as he crosses the lobby
and enters
the XIVth century.

I follow him as far
as the room with the blue Madonnas.

And Counting

(*Bellagio, Italy*)

Well of course I'm not worth it but neither is
the Taj Mahal for that matter so who's counting?
Someone's got to listen to the fountain;
someone is due to catch the *nymphaea tuberosa*
closing promptly five till five. Opulence
breathes on its own a little better
if there's a gardener raking or a scholar
primed to record its suscitation. I came here

to write, knock a few poems off the ledger
of accounts payable—only to discover
pasta put me under just as neatly as sambuca
would catapult me into telepathic communication. So
I took a few day trips, sprained an ankle on the courts,
fell asleep over Catullus-*cum*-Zukofsky . . . in

short, nothing happened that wasn't unexceptional,
but that's the crux of moral implication, is it not?
Mother Mary, ingénue with the golden womb,
you would not comprehend how cruel a modern game of
tennis is: you only had one phosphorescent ball.
Here's a riddle for Our Age: when the sky's the limit,
how can you tell you've gone too far?

DIALECTICAL ROMANCE

He asked if she believed in God
so she looked him in the eye
before answering No but he wouldn't
give in: Not even a little bit?
Then because it was raining and
they were walking down a path others
might have called paradise, she added
Not even a little—though at times
she wished she could. It was a lie
but she was being polite; besides,
they had just turned from Suicide Point
and it seemed the social thing to say.

He believed there was a force but didn't feel
compelled to give it a name; it needn't be
embodied. She thought of the Virgin
at Bergamo, marble limbs dressed in dusty
crinolines, a life-sized Barbie doll.

Some force has to have made all this—
his armsweep sending more droplets down,
gravel protesting like gritting teeth—
and then set everything loose in it.

So God's given up? she ventured, which made him
swallow. Remembering where they'd been, then,
those soaked crags and lake-stunned altitudes,
she dredged up for his sake a comparison
from computers: a program so large
there could be no answer
except in working it through.

MEDUSA

I've got to go
down where my eye
can't reach
hairy star
who forgets to shiver
forgets the cool suck
inside

Someday long
off someone will
see me
fling me up
until I hook
into sky

drop his memory

My hair
dry water

In a Neutral City

Someday we'll talk about the day lily,
the puff dandelion aloof on its milky stalk,
wild birds defying notation. Someday
the last sad trickle in a toilet stall
will recall fountains sighing into themselves
and ant-freckled stones
swept clean with a breath. In rain

over lunch we will search for a topic
only to remember a hill, a path hushed
in the waxen shade of magnolias.
Someday we'll talk because there'll be
little else to say:
and then the cheese and pears will arrive,
and the worms.

V

> ... Don't hope for things elsewhere.
> Now that you've wasted your life here, in this small corner,
> you've destroyed it everywhere in the world.

—CAVAFY

S A I N T S

She used to pull them
from herself and count:
Have mercy, have mercy—
blackeyed peas flicked into a pot.

Why go out into the sunshine
and blustery azaleas, why leave
this overcrowded bed?
She's fat now, she stinks in warm weather.
She'll pin on a hat, groan into a pew,
spend the hour watching stained glass
swirl through Michael's boat
like holy water.

Between her knees, each had been
a neat hunger,
each one a freedom.
So many now, perishing under the rafters!
They are like the tin replicas of eyes and limbs
hung up in small churches,
meticulous
cages, medallions
swinging in the dazed air.

GENIE'S PRAYER UNDER THE KITCHEN SINK

*Housebuilding was conceived as a heroic effort
to stop time, suspend decay and interrupt the
ordained flow to ruin that started with
Adam's fall.*

—*from* House *by Tracy Kidder*

Hair and bacon grease, pearl button
popped in the search for a shawl, smashed radiant aluminum
foil, blunt shreds of wax paper—
nothing gets lost, you can't flush the shit
without it floating back in the rheumy eye of the bowl
or coagulating in the drop-belly of transitional pipes.
And who gets to drag his bad leg
into the kitchen and under the sink,
flashlight scattering roaches, rusted brillo pads
his earned divan?

            The hot water squeezed
to a trickle so she counted out the finger holes
and dialed her least-loved son.
I don't believe in stepping
in the goddam shoes of any other man
but I came because I'm good at this, I'm good

with my hands; last March I bought some 2 by 4s
at Home Depot and honed them down
to the sleekest, blondest, free-standing bar
any mildewed basement in a cardboard housing tract
under the glass gloom of a factory clock
ever saw. I put the best bottles
behind it: Dimple scotch, crystal Gordon,

one mean nigger rye. I stacked the records.
Called two girls who like to perform on shag rugs,
spun my mirrored globe and watched.

They were sweet, like pet monkeys. I know
Mom called me over so I'd have to lurch up
the porch steps and she could click her tongue
and say, That's what you get for evil living. Christ,
she took in wash through fourteen children and
he left her every time, went off on a 9-month binge
while the ripening babies ate her rich thighs
to sticks.

 I was the last one; I'm Genie,
Eugene June Bug; the others made me
call them "Aunt" and "Uncle" in public.
All except Annalee—cancer screwed *her.*
She withered like my leg. She dragged her body
through the house like a favorite doll.

Yes, I'm a man born too late for
Ain't-that-a-shame, I'm a monkey
with a message and a heart like
my father who fell laughing to his knees
when it burst and 24 crows spilled
from his mouth and they were all named Jim.

When I'm finished here
I'm gonna build a breezeway next,
with real nice wicker on some astroturf.

THE GORGE

I.

Little Cuyahoga's done up left town.
No one saw it leaving.
No one saw it leaving

Though it left a twig or two,
And a snaky line of rotting
Fish, a dead man's shoes,

Gnats, scarred pocket-
Books, a rusted garden nozzle,
Rats and crows. April

In bone and marrow. Soaked
With sugary dogwood, the gorge floats
In the season's morass,

Remembering its walnut, its hickory,
Its oak, its elm,
Its sassafras. Ah,

II.

April's arthritic magnitude!
Little Joe ran away
From the swollen man

On the porch, ran across
The muck to the railroad track.
Lost his penny and sat

Right down by the rail,
There where his father
Couldn't see him crying.

That's why the express
Stayed on the track.
That's why a man

On a porch shouted out
Because his son forgot
His glass of iced water. That's

Why they carried little Joe
Home and why his toe
Ain't never coming back. Oh

III.

This town reeks mercy.
This gorge leaves a trail
Of anecdotes,

The poor man's history.

CANARY

for Michael S. Harper

Billie Holiday's burned voice
had as many shadows as lights,
a mournful candelabra against a sleek piano,
the gardenia her signature under that ruined face.

(Now you're cooking, drummer to bass,
magic spoon, magic needle.
Take all day if you have to
with your mirror and your bracelet of song.)

Fact is, the invention of women under siege
has been to sharpen love in the service of myth.

If you can't be free, be a mystery.

The Island Women of Paris

skim from curb to curb like regatta,
from Pont Neuf to the Quai de la Rappe
in cool negotiation with traffic,
each a country to herself
transposed to this city
by a fluke called "imperial courtesy."

The island women glide past held aloft
by a wire running straight to heaven.
Who can ignore their ornamental bearing,
turbans haughty as parrots,
or deft braids carved into airy cages
transfixed on their manifest brows?

The island women move through Paris
as if they had just finished inventing
their destinations. It's better
not to get in their way. And better
not look an island woman in the eye—
unless you like feeling unnecessary.

À L'Opéra

A friend, blonde pigtail flung over an ear,
consoles her with cheek kisses.
They take no notice of the police
ranged down the steps in two lanes
from the marbled interior
where a delegation is
happening—someone famous, perhaps.

More friends arrive. Of them the boys,
correct in their flannels, kiss her too,
and with the ironic grace of the French
take her briefly to their chests.

Now the police block off the boulevard,
traffic snorting at their backs;
and though I wait for fifteen minutes
in the doorway of a corner café
no dignitary ever descends,
nor does she stop crying.

Obbligato

Consider that I have loved you for forty-nine years, that I
have loved you since childhood despite the storms that
have wasted my life. . . . I have loved you, I love you and
will continue to love you, and I am sixty-one years old, I
know the world and have no illusions.

—Hector Berlioz to Madame F.

Patrons talk and talk and nothing
comes. His thighs shift, the cup flies
sending dish and creamed tea
spinning, a corona of perfect disgrace.

The murmured solicitudes, the gloves.

He could debate the existence of God, describe
the vexed look on the face of the timpanist
who had never heard of felt-tips. Or the trumpets
failing their entrance in *Iphegenie*—

I fear I suffer from poplar blossoms,
so profuse this season.

The entire summer he was twelve she wore pink shoes.

Invisible command, the enemy everywhere.

LINT

Beneath the brushed wing of the mallard
an awkward loveliness.

Under the cedar lid a mirror
and a box in a box.

Blue is all around
like an overturned bowl.

What to do with this noise
and persistent lint,

the larder filled past caring?
How good to revolve

on the edge of a system—
small, unimaginable, cold.

The Royal Workshops

1

Stone kettles on the beach by Sidon.
Salt and slime, colorless juice:
murex brandaris,
murex trunculus,
simmering.

Two kettles
on the salt beach:
dark red,
dark blue.

2

By the sign of his hand
you shall know him, holy slave.
By the litmus mark on his earlobe
you shall know the Jew, the wretched dyer.

3

Zebulun wails:
I received only mountains &
hills, oceans & rivers.

God replies:
Because of the purple snail
all will be in need of your service.

Zebulun says:
You gave my brother countries;
me you gave the snail!

God answers:
After all, I made them dependent on you
for the snail.

4

A slave practised in the labor
of red-purple and blue
was sent from Tyre to the Temple
to ferment an unpierceable scrim.

5

The Romans had their Jews,
the Greeks their Abyssinians—
red-haired Thaddaeus,
blue-skinned Muhammed.

6

Slave's work, to wring and dry and drape;
man's work to adorn the unspeakable.
Evening lavishes shade on a cold battlefield
as God retreats

before a fanfare of trumpets and heliotrope.

ON THE ROAD TO DAMASCUS

And it came to pass, that, as I made my
journey, and was come nigh unto Damascus
about noon, suddenly there shone from heaven
a great light round about me. And I fell to the
ground . . .

Acts 22:6-7

They say I was struck down by the voice of an angel:
    flames poured through the radiant fabric of heaven
as I cried out and fell to my knees.

My first recollection was of Unbroken Blue—
    but two of the guards have already sworn by
the tip of my tongue set ablaze. As an official,

I recognize the lure of a good story:
    useless to suggest that my mount
had stumbled, that I was pitched into a clump

of wild chamomile, its familiar stink
    soothing even as my palms sprang blisters
under the nicked leaves. I heard shouts,

the horse pissing in terror—but my eyes
    had dropped to my knees, and I saw nothing.
I was a Roman and had my business

among the clouded towers of Damascus.
    I had not counted on earth rearing,
honey streaming down a parched sky,

a spear skewering me to the dust of the road
   on the way to the city I would never
enter now, her markets steaming with vendors

and compatriots in careless armor lifting a hand
   in greeting as they call out my name,
only to find no one home.

Old Folk's Home, Jerusalem

for Harry Timar

Evening, the bees fled, the honeysuckle
in its golden dotage, all the sickrooms ajar.
Law of the Innocents: What doesn't end, sloshes over . . .
even here, where destiny girds the cucumber.

So you wrote a few poems. The horned
thumbnail hooked into an ear doesn't care.
The gray underwear wadded over a belt says So what.

The night air is minimalist,
a needlepoint with raw moon as signature.
In this desert the question's not
Can you see? but *How far off?*
Valley settlements put on their lights
like armor; there's finch chit and my sandal's
inconsequential crunch.

Everyone waiting here was once in love.

About the Author

RITA DOVE was born in Akron, Ohio, in 1952. She has received numerous awards for her writing: the Lavan Younger Poets' Prize from the Academy of American Poets; the General Electric Foundation Award; and a Guggenheim Fellowship, among others. In 1987 she received the Pulitzer Prize for her third book of poems, *Thomas and Beulah.*

Ms. Dove teaches creative writing at the University of Virginia.